Contents

The German pilot Baron von Richthofen was the top First World War **flying ace**. He shot down 80 aircraft. He was called the 'Red Baron' because his planes were red.

What's Inside

Planes

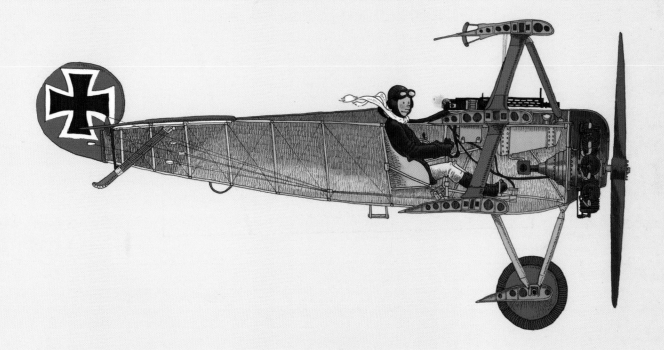

W

FRANKLIN WATTS

Franklin Watts
Published in paperback in 2018 by The Watts Publishing Group

Designed and illustrated by David West

Dewey number 629.1'3334
PB ISBN 978 1 4451 6347 5

Printed in Malaysia

Franklin Watts
An imprint of
Hachette Children's Group
Part of The Watts Publishing Group
Carmelite House
50 Victoria Embankment
London EC4Y 0DZ

An Hachette UK Company
www.hachette.co.uk

www.franklinwatts.co.uk

WHAT'S INSIDE PLANES
was produced for Franklin Watts by
David West ⚇ Children's Books, 6 Princeton Court, 55 Felsham Road, London SW15 1AZ

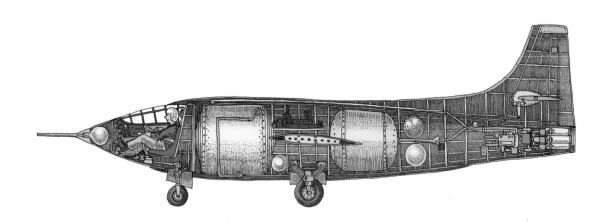

The First Planes

The first planes were made of canvas stretched over wooden and metal frames. They usually had two pairs of wings. Some, like this Fokker Dr. 1 triplane, had three pairs of wings. These First World War (1914–18) planes had machine guns to shoot down enemy planes.

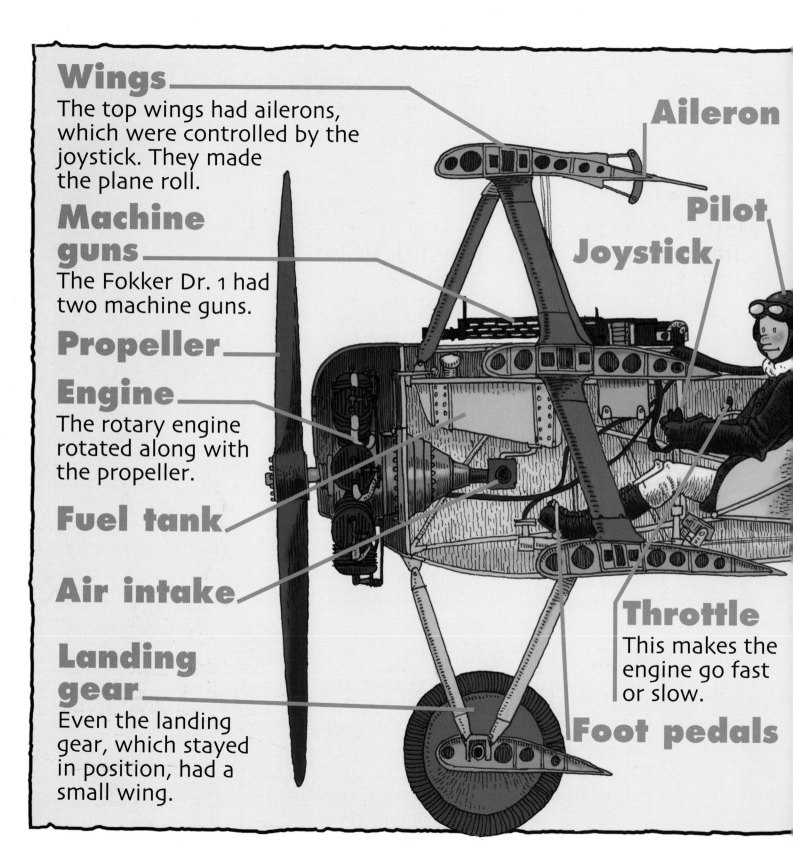

Wings

The top wings had ailerons, which were controlled by the joystick. They made the plane roll.

Machine guns

The Fokker Dr. 1 had two machine guns.

Propeller

Engine

The rotary engine rotated along with the propeller.

Fuel tank

Air intake

Landing gear

Even the landing gear, which stayed in position, had a small wing.

Aileron

Pilot

Joystick

Throttle

This makes the engine go fast or slow.

Foot pedals

Fokker Dr. 1

Metal frame
Most of the plane had a frame made of aluminium tubes.

Tail plane
The tail plane's elevator was controlled by the joystick, which made the plane go up or down.

Tail skid

Canvas skin
The metal frame and wings were covered in canvas, which was then painted.

Rudder
The rudder was controlled by foot pedals and turned the plane left or right. This is known as **yaw**.

Flying Boats

Flying boats were planes that could land and take off on water. They were used between 1918 and 1940 to ferry passengers, freight and mail. They could fly long distances across the Atlantic and Pacific oceans, offering passengers luxury travel. This Boeing 314 Clipper could carry 77 passengers and had a maximum speed of 303 kph (188 mph).

The Boeing 314 Clippers had a lounge and dining area. White-coated stewards served six-course meals with gleaming silver service.

Cockpit
The pilot and co-pilot flew the plane from the cockpit on the upper deck.

Navigation room
The navigator and radio operator worked in this room.

Engine
The Boeing 314 had four engines.

Cargo hold

Dining room
Passengers were served fine meals in the dining room.

Pilot

Crew's day cabin

Stabiliser

Washroom
These planes had a washroom with a toilet, like modern airliners.

Fuel reservoir
Fuel was stored in the wings and the stabiliser.

Boeing 314 Clipper

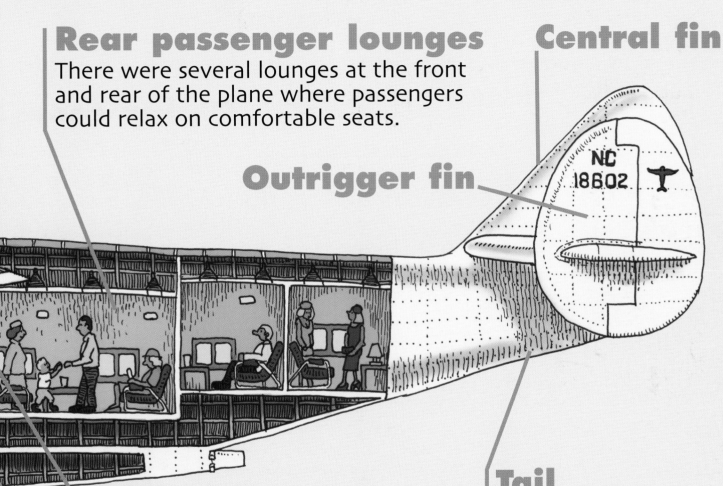

Rear passenger lounges

There were several lounges at the front and rear of the plane where passengers could relax on comfortable seats.

Central fin

Outrigger fin

NC 18602

Crew's quarters

Sleeping cabin

Some of the lounges could be converted to sleeping cabins. There were also fold-down beds on some flights.

Tail

The tail of the Boeing 314 had three fins; one central fin and two outrigger fins.

The B-17 was known as the 'Flying Fortress'. This was because of the many machine guns pointing out in every direction to protect it from enemy fighter planes.

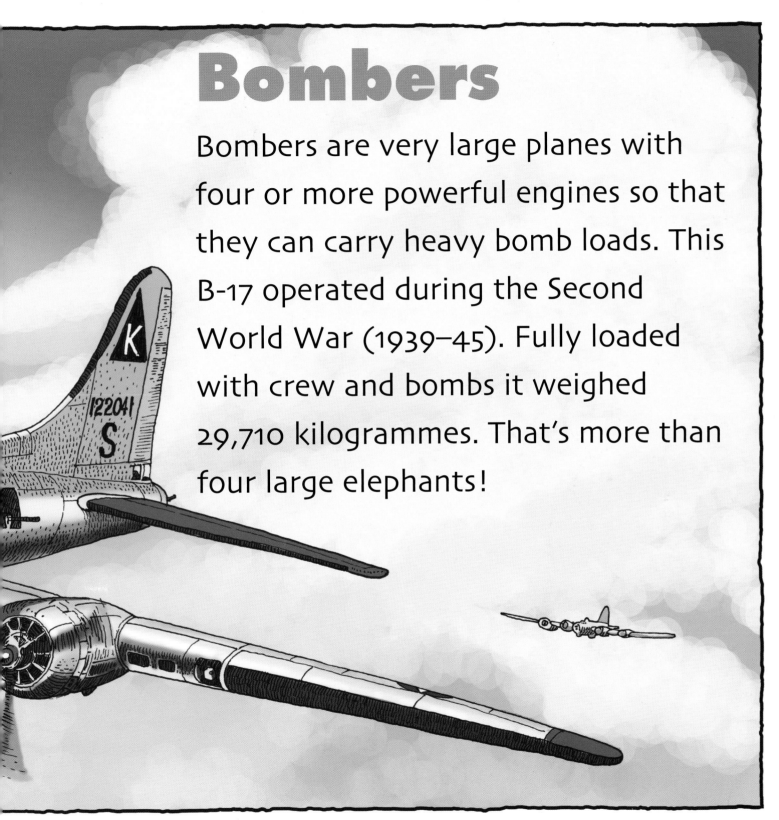

Bombers

Bombers are very large planes with four or more powerful engines so that they can carry heavy bomb loads. This B-17 operated during the Second World War (1939–45). Fully loaded with crew and bombs it weighed 29,710 kilogrammes. That's more than four large elephants!

B-17 Flying Fortress

Bombardier
This crew member aimed the bombs. He also operated the forward machine guns.

Pilots
The plane was flown by the pilot and the co-pilot.

Dorsal gun turret

Radio operator
He used the radio to keep in touch with other planes and ground control.

Navigator
The navigator plotted the course for the pilots.

Engine
The B-17 was powered by four large engines that gave it a top speed of 462 kph (287 mph).

Bomb bay
The B-17 could carry 7,983 kilogrammes of bombs.

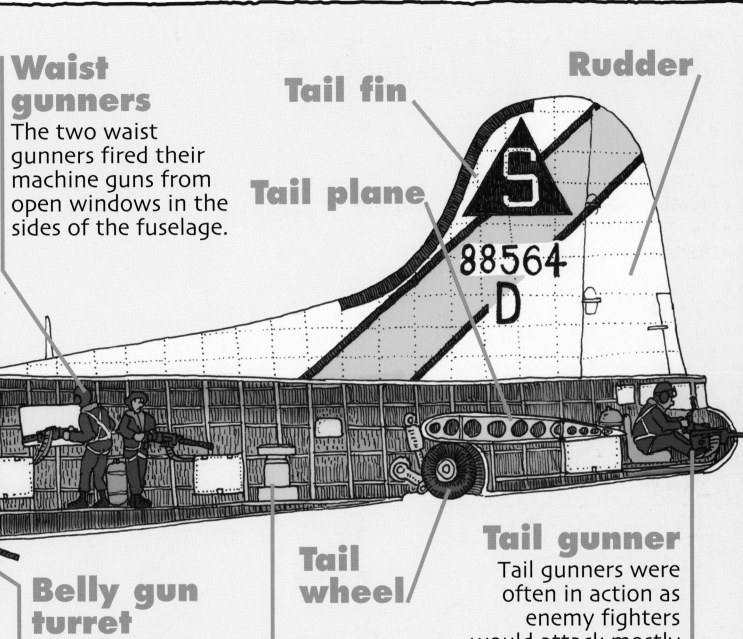

Waist gunners

The two waist gunners fired their machine guns from open windows in the sides of the fuselage.

Tail fin

Tail plane

Rudder

88564
D

Belly gun turret

This crew member sat in a self-contained drum on the underside, which had twin machine guns.

Tail wheel

Toilet

Tail gunner

Tail gunners were often in action as enemy fighters would attack mostly from the rear.

The Bell X-1 was launched from a B-29 Superfortress bomber. After it made its record-breaking flight, the Bell X-1 glided back to land on a dry lake bed.

Supersonic Planes

On October 14, 1947, Captain Charles 'Chuck' Yeager became the first person to go faster than the speed of sound – approximately 1,235 kph (768 mph). He did it in an experimental rocket plane called the Bell X-1.

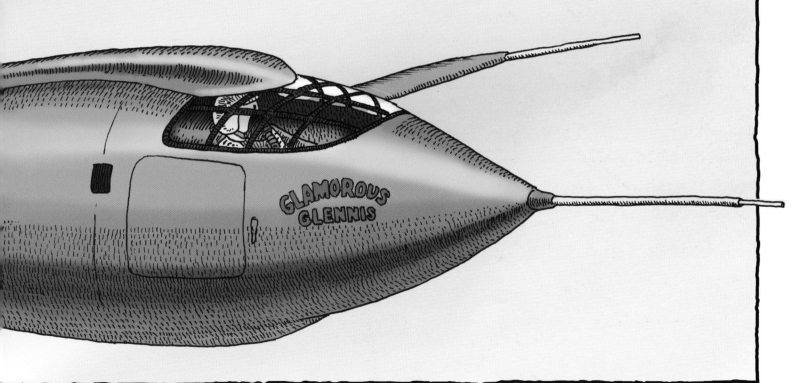

Bell X-1

Cockpit
The cockpit was small and had to be entered through a door at the side.

Liquid oxygen tank
Liquid oxygen was stored in a pressurised tank. It was mixed with the fuel to be burned by the rocket engines.

Wing

Door

Pilot

Nosewheel

Main landing gear
Two main wheels and a nose wheel were lowered during landing.

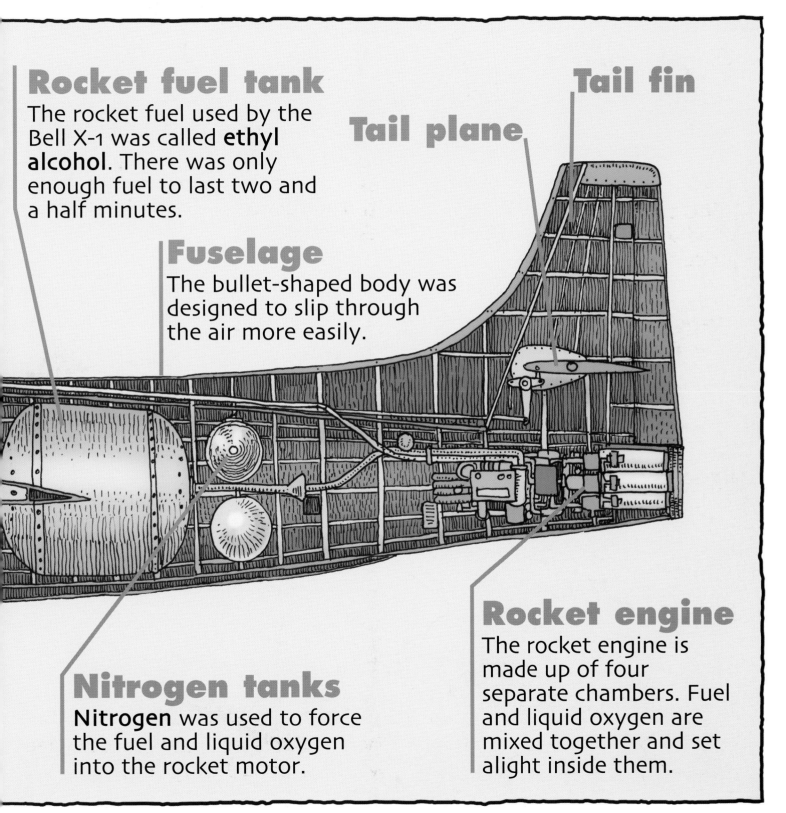

Rocket fuel tank

The rocket fuel used by the Bell X-1 was called **ethyl alcohol**. There was only enough fuel to last two and a half minutes.

Tail plane

Tail fin

Fuselage

The bullet-shaped body was designed to slip through the air more easily.

Nitrogen tanks

Nitrogen was used to force the fuel and liquid oxygen into the rocket motor.

Rocket engine

The rocket engine is made up of four separate chambers. Fuel and liquid oxygen are mixed together and set alight inside them.

Private jets are also called business jets. Their passenger cabins are often luxurious, decked out with bedrooms, TV lounges and even bathrooms with gold taps.

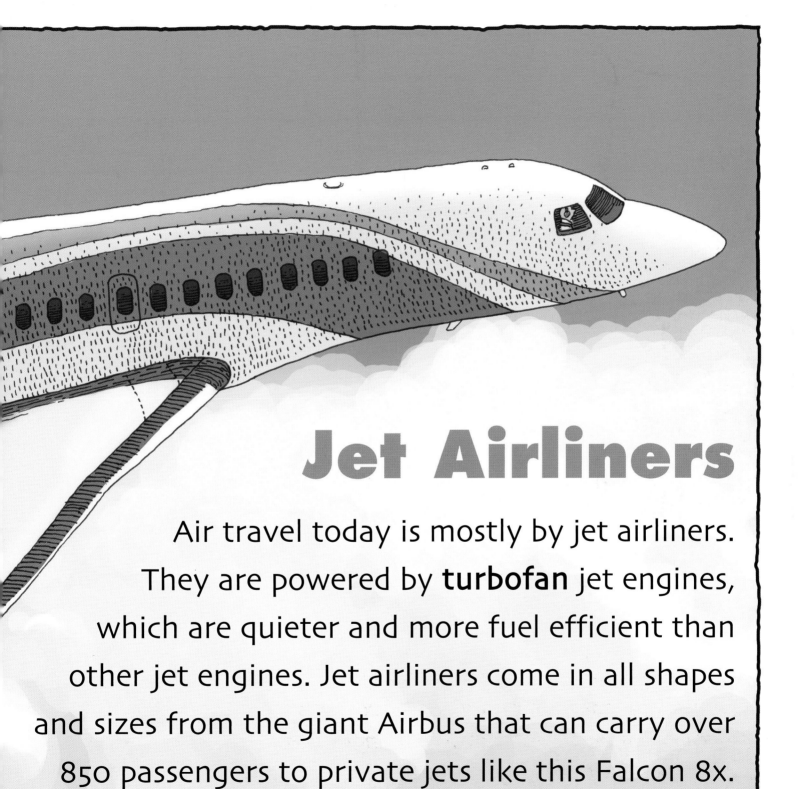

Jet Airliners

Air travel today is mostly by jet airliners. They are powered by **turbofan** jet engines, which are quieter and more fuel efficient than other jet engines. Jet airliners come in all shapes and sizes from the giant Airbus that can carry over 850 passengers to private jets like this Falcon 8x.

Falcon 8x

Cockpit
The pilot and co-pilot fly the plane aided by computers.

Galley
A kitchen at the front supplies hot food and drinks for the passengers.

Passenger cabin
The passengers sit in comfort and listen to music, watch TV and play computer games.

Weather radar

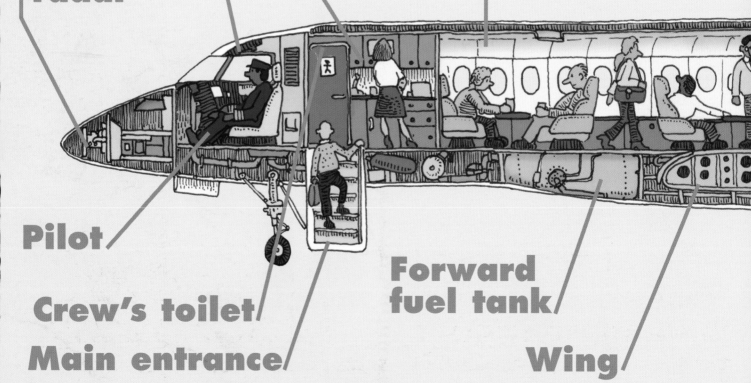

Pilot

Crew's toilet

Main entrance

Forward fuel tank

Wing

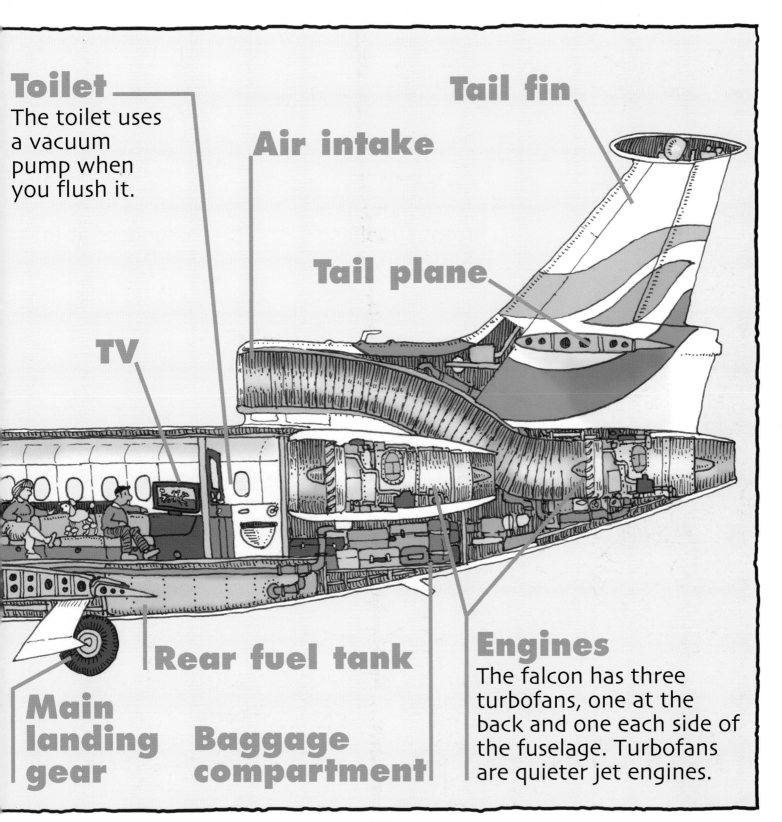

Toilet
The toilet uses a vacuum pump when you flush it.

Air intake

Tail fin

Tail plane

TV

Engines
The falcon has three turbofans, one at the back and one each side of the fuselage. Turbofans are quieter jet engines.

Rear fuel tank

Main landing gear

Baggage compartment

Glossary

ethyl alcohol
A colourless, flammable liquid, also called ethanol, grain alcohol, or alcohol.

flying ace
A fighter pilot that has shot down five or more planes.

nitrogen
A gas that makes up 78 per cent of Earth's atmosphere. It can be compressed and stored in tanks.

turbofan
A jet engine with a large fan at its front. The large fan pushes air around the jet engine. This provides thrust and a layer of insulation around the jet engine, which reduces noise.

yaw
A rotational movement of an aircraft that makes it turn left or right.

Index